EDINBURGH

— the tramway years

ALAN W. BROTCHIE

ISBNo   0   905069   12   9

Published by
N.B. TRACTION GROUP
31 FORFAR ROAD, DUNDEE

£1.50

Above: **Edinburgh trams had an undisguised "presence" — dignified and totally in keeping with their role in the capital city. Car 30 is at the Waterloo Place terminus of cars for Portobello, Joppa, Musselburgh and Levenhall, and was photographed in 1937. A short length of cable-tramway track has been reinstated near this spot to commemorate tramway days.**

Cover: **Car 221, one of Edinburgh's last trams, drops passengers at the foot of the Mound. The evening sun highlights the Royal Scottish Academy and silhouettes the Old Town sky line.**

INTRODUCTION

"Edinburgh — the Tramway Years" has been put together in an attempt to recall the atmosphere of the City's streets in the times before they were given over entirely to the internal combustion engine. Although the city has so far been spared the major intrusion of an Inner-Relief road, there have been many changes to streets and roads — but on a smaller scale.

The period covered (1871-1956) showed but little physical change in street architecture, with the probable major exception of the block now containing the North British Hotel — but in the years following 1956 there have been major brash alterations. Previously, the most noticeable change through the passing years was in transportation — from horse tram to cable, then electric; from walking, through the horse-drawn to the horseless era. There were other more subtle changes — gas lamps to electric, setts to asphalt. Nobody could think that all the changes have been for the worse; old slums have gone, but new ones have been created.

The photographic selection is purely personal and it has been deliberately concentrated upon scenes from post-1945, scenes which are to me memorable. Earlier views are included to form a transport record of these years which are still remembered by others. One great difficulty in Edinburgh, of course, is to find photographs which are *not* of Princes Street, the Royal Mile, or the Castle, and an effort has been made to present a wider view. Many of these scenes were not taken with a view to recording an animated street scene, and in many cases the interest is incidental to the reason for taking a particular photograph.

Almost twenty-five years have passed since Edinburgh's last tram ran through the streets of the city, and there is now a strong feeling that a Light-rail transport system would greatly assist the present public transport requirements. Many Continental cities did not scrap their tramways in the 1950s and today they have modern, fast urban transport — electrically operated and without dependence on imported fuels.

Aberdour, Fife.   May 1979.

Waiting for your car — often wet, usually windy, but seldom long — outside Macvitties at the West End.

An 1880's record of unhurried Princes Street life. The south side of the street has now changed drastically, with the North British Hotel replacing the old buildings, and the formal roof garden above Waverley Market replaced by a desolate car park.

The West End of Princes Street c. 1890, with a well laden horse brake — the "Dalmeny" — returning from a trip to view the wonder of the age, the new Forth Railway Bridge. On the earliest horse trams the outside seats were back-to-back, or "knifeboard" style.

Horse trams came to Edinburgh in 1871, and routes were quickly added, including one up to the "South Side" in 1872. Edinburgh's hills demanded that instead of the usual two horses, on occasions three or even four were necessary. This 1890's view of the University from Surgeon's Hall shows the extra "trace" horse which will be taken off at the top of the incline.

Horse cars ran from Tollcross to High Street, by the Tron Church. This scene, from May 1898, shows Cockburn Street — and the "Myoscopic Show: Animated Photographic Pictures by Electric Light" — between the butcher-meat emporium and the offices of the Equitable Loan Company. The horse car (number 101) is one of several purchased from the Glasgow Tramways Company.

Horse tramways could not serve the steeper streets and a separate undertaking (the Edinburgh Northern Tramways Coy.) opened cable hauled routes from Princes Street to Goldenacre and Comely Bank. This view, taken in 1892, shows one of the earliest cars, number 3, at Canonmills Bridge. The old toll-house on the right has long disappeared.

The second cable tram route was from Frederick Street to Comely Bank Avenue via Stockbridge, where this view was taken c. 1895. A line off to the right connected the two lines with the Power Station and depot in Henderson Row. The buildings on the left have now been replaced by new flats.

Four power stations (each with car sheds attached) eventually served 26 miles of cable tramway. That at Tollcross (seen here c. 1900) was a handsome red sandstone building which was used later by electric trams and finally buses until demolished recently.

At Coltbridge (Roseburn) the local "Bobby" and message boy both stand to attention for the photographer. After reconstruction for cable operation the line was extended to Murrayfield.

Nether Liberton cable tram terminus photographed (as was the scene above) in 1905. An electric tramway was planned, but never built, passing to the left of the old cottages to serve Eskbank, Dalkeith and Bonnyrigg.

The cable system, particularly in its later years, became prone to breakdown, and when this happened it was necessary to stop the cable and thus immobilise all cars served. This Princes Street scene shows just this event — all cars stranded but remaining the regulation distance apart. The drivers have gathered at car 189 to discuss the problem.

One common difficulty was when one strand of the wire rope frayed and unwrapped, usually in the most awkward manner. To effect repair the splicing gang were called out — specialists in dealing with the 3 7/8 inch circumference cable. This scene shows them dealing with the cause of the hold-up above.

Leith Corporation opened their own self-contained electric tramway system in August 1905. This view, taken not long after, at Pier Place, Newhaven, shows three of the new cars by the Marine Hotel. At this time the line to Granton had not been built.

The harbour of the fiercely independent fishing village of Newhaven. The open top Leith Corporation tram is passing old cottages which have recently been removed, although many others have been restored.

A cable tram route was opened up Marchmont Road in May 1900, and this quiet scene shows car 166 on the 6 service. James Gillespie's boys' school occupies the centre with, to the right, Marchmont Crescent.

Cable car route 2 ran from Pilrig to Gorgie. In this view of Gorgie Road with tram number 107, can be seen the overhead poles at the foot of Ardmillan Terrace for the Slateford electric route.

A later (1908) cable line was built in Broughton Street, linking the two original Northern Company routes to the rest of the system. Car 47 was built by the Tramway Company that year.

Edinburgh had to make do with a short suburban branch tramway as its first electric traction experiment. This ran 1¼ miles from Slateford to meet the cable line at Ardmillan. In this pre-First World War scene is electrified cable car 38 and, on the left, top-hatted mourners at North Merchiston cemetery.

One of the longest cable routes was from Waterloo Place, by Portobello where the power house was, to Joppa. Car 220 is approaching the terminus to connect with the waiting electric tram of the independent Musselburgh Tramways Company, running as far as Port Seton. Photographed 1912.

The official car (number 123) opening Edinburgh Corporation's electrified lines on 20th June 1922 was besieged by students as it passed the University. On the left in this scene at Nicolson Square is cable car 35.

A joint service was inaugurated over the Musselburgh Company lines, via Musselburgh to Port Seton. Company car 11 shows clearly the offset trolley.

Edinburgh did not use their newest cars on the indifferent track of the Company line. This is a rebuilt cable car, number 52, at the Marine Tea House, Port Seton terminus.

To avoid any demonstration to mark the passing of the last cable car, the transition was made, without ceremony, during Saturday 23rd June 1923. Electric car 12 (rebuilt from a cable car) is here on the replacing service. Cable car 217 was rebuilt to run a further twenty years as a similar electric car.

The Craiglockhart cable line was extended in March 1926 to Colinton. This sylvan scene at the top of Craiglockhart Avenue shows the encroaching bungalow development. Car 3, built in 1927, was re-numbered 75 in February 1935 and rebuilt with the top deck ends enclosed.

The George Street tramway was built as a by-pass for Princes Street, but was little used. Car 217 is on route 24 from Comely Bank which came in to town in this direction, then looped back along Princes Street and Frederick Street.

At the top of Marchmont Road, car 22 is about to reverse on a short working of route 6 back to Waverley.

On 1st June 1929 car 349 ran out of control down Liberton Brae and overturned in the garden of number 40 after leaving the track. None of the four passengers was injured.

A busy West End scene in the mid twenties. Horse traffic is now outnumbered by motor vehicles, but several horse cabs wait outside Maule's shop. Most of the trams are reconstructed cable cars, but 265 at the loading island is ex-Leith Corporation number 35.

For rugby internationals at Murrayfield an intensive service was operated from St Andrew Square, and during the match specials waited at the outer end of the Corstorphine line, which was served temporarily by a bus.

New ideas were continually developed by the Corporation Tramway Department, culminating in the "£4,000 tram", number 180, placed in service in 1932. Its bright red and grey livery earned it the name "Red Biddy".

The Comely Bank route (number 24) was one of the shortest in length and was also the first to be abandoned. Little, other than removal of the trams has altered this 1935 scene at Stockbridge.

Decorated cars were a frequent feature of pre-war years. Car 221 was painted silver and posed in St Andrew Square while advertising an R.A.F. exhibition in Waverley Market in February 1939.

War conditions imposed restrictions on operation, although generally Edinburgh fared much better than many other cities. Car 370 came to grief after a confrontation with an S.M.T. bus in Portobello. Netting on the windows and obscured headlamps made vehicles difficult to see, so steps and fenders were painted white.

After the war a return to normal was made as quickly as possible, and the familiar route lights were reintroduced. A simplified and uniform livery was adopted. This windy scene at the foot of the Mound in 1949 typifies these days. The Princes Street frontages have changed drastically.

The outpost at Granton, formerly part of the Leith system, was the terminus of no less than eight routes. For Stenhouse route 2 ran by Lower Granton Road.

Also serving Stenhouse was route 3 from Newington or Liberton Dams. At the foot of Ardmillan Terrace the Slateford tracks branch off to the right; behind, the typical Edinburgh tenements of Dalry Road.

Leith Street in the 50s; prior to destruction of the north side to allow replacement by the St James' Centre and Hotel. The contrast between the level stability of Princes Street and the drop down between grimy 19th century tenements with pubs, dance halls and small shops was very noticeable. The left side of the street still stands — but now derelict awaiting development.

Nicolson Street and South Bridge is still a busy shopping artery. This view from Surgeon's Hall takes in the Old College dome and facade, Blair's drapery and the Empire Theatre, then giving twice nightly variety programmes. In 1954 the star turn advertised was Phyllis Dixey, well known strip tease artiste, on her annual visit.

After the war Edinburgh purchased a batch of cars from Manchester Corporation. This one, Manchester 196, later Edinburgh 403, was photographed near Hillend being delivered. They were designed by R. Stuart Pilcher who masterminded Edinburgh's cable to electric change-over before becoming Manchester's Transport Manager.

These eleven cars were only operated on the route from Waterloo Place to Levenhall via Musselburgh. This scene with cars 410 (Manchester 349) and 402 (676) is near Levenhall terminus, where there is now a large roundabout on the busy A1 trunk road.

Cars from Waterloo Place ran down Regent Road, passing the Royal High School. These buildings were refurbished for use by the proposed Scottish Assembly. A crop of parking meters has replaced the trees.

At Abbey Church the Regent Road and London Road lines separated. Services for termini other than Waterloo Place took to the right, joining the procession of cars from Leith at Elm Row.

The roadway at this narrow part of Musselburgh High Street has since been widened. Car 175, built by the Corporation in 1934, is heading for Levenhall terminus.

Route 1, Liberton to Corstorphine, lasted until 28th March 1954. Car 230 was photographed at "Western Corner", the junction of Saughtonhall Drive and Corstorphine Road, with S.M.T. Leyland J46 en route to Pumpherston.

The buses which took over on the 1 route were often older than the trams; this 1943 Daimler (DWS472) is on the replacing 31 route. Tram 106 in this view of Shandwick Place is a special running to the Zoo, prior to close down of this route in July 1954.

The Heart of Midlothian F.C. memorial clock at Haymarket, with Haymarket Station beyond. The "crow-step" gable of the Old Haymarket Inn matches those of the newer "Ryries" pub adjacent.

Corstorphine village, looking east along St John's Road. Car 115 on route 25 was photographed in April 1954, three months before closure came.

The bend between North St Andrew Street and York Place was banked to aid trams round the curve. Car 261 is another "one-off", built by the Corporation at Shrubhill in 1932. Behind is the National Museum of Antiquities of Scotland.

"The Quatermass Xperiment" is the main attraction at the Palace, Foot of Leith Walk. Car 369 on route 17 from Granton to Newington Station is leaving Constitution Street to cross Edinburgh's most complex tramway junction — most of it disused — a legacy from Leith Corporation.

At the top of Leith Street, with St James' Street leading to St James' Square behind (where the Transport Department offices were located). This scene from 1952 has changed greatly in recent years.

Broughton Street with the Theatre Royal and St Mary's R.C. Cathedral. From this view, only the Cathedral remains. The narrow street has completely disappeared, as have all the buildings behind.

Similarly nothing remains today to identify this scene, looking up Leith Street. The left side has been cleared and the right is now Lewis's store.

Car 223 in York Place, with the fanciful skyline of St Paul's and St George's Episcopal Church behind. Leyland 423 is on service 22 which replaced and extended former tram service 2.

"Gayfield Square", or Antigua Street island, for passengers travelling north to Pilrig or Leith. These centre poles were originally erected by Leith Corporation along Great Junction Street.

Ferry Road at Allan Street; not greatly changed but the tall poles with Leith Corporation's coat-of-arms on the base have been replaced by an uninspired concrete design. Car 20 is en route to the terminus of route 7 in Craighall Road.

Newhaven Main Street is now by-passed, but these old outside-stair fisherfolk's houses remain. The pole-painter has just been busy here.

Traffic jams in Earl Grey Street at Tollcross in the 1950s. These did not disappear — as had been confidently predicted — when the trams were removed, and eventually the whole right hand side of the street was demolished. Now most of the left side is derelict, and the area has changed from a busy community to a windy expanse.

Snowy scene on Colinton Road near the Barracks entrance — high speeds were often achieved here when few stops were required.

An attractive view on the same route, with car 233 reflected in the waters of the Union Canal near Craiglockhart Station.

The Colinton line joined the other routes at Gilmore Place. The King's Theatre and Tarvit Street can be seen beyond. Car 195 was usually a "Portobello" car, not often on these routes.

At the G.P.O. junction with car 172 making for Princes Street and Corstorphine. JWS582 is a refurbished former London bus purchased to facilitate tramway replacement, running on former tram route 3 to Stenhouse.

Looking towards Arthur's Seat from Liberton terminus with car 226. The double track layout was for the mile long extension authorised to Kaimes, which was postponed in 1939 on the outbreak of war, and not revived afterwards.

A special service for visitors to the Royal Infirmary was run from Hanover Street at appropriate times. Car 193 waits for its starting time.

South Bridge in the last years of the trams, with many well-known small shops, and a constant procession of trams.

The junction of South Clerk Street and Preston Street, with Car 45 on route 5, and 164 on the 14 circle to Churchhill.

Snow still covers Arthur's Seat, but it has almost disappeared from the streets. Car 265 in Grange Road at Cumin Place on service 14.

Car 187 climbs Morningside Road towards the Churchhill junction. The state of the track and road surface is typical of latter-day maintenance.

The pillars at the ends of Melville Drive were erected for the 1886 Exhibition held on the Meadows; Marchmont Circle car 237 in August 1953.

Lothian Road at the Usher Hall loading island, April 1955. The Western Approach Road now joins here after passing through the former Caley Goods Yard on the left. Car 47 is heading for Bernard Street on route 16. The "island" was then served by seven services.

The terminus for Morningside Station cars (routes 5 and 23) is off to the right here at Belhaven Terrace. This busy junction is now a labyrinth of traffic lights. Car 250 on the left is one of ten supplied by R. Y. Pickering of Wishaw in 1932.

The long pull up Pitt Street and Dundas Street to George Street – the reason for introduction of the first of Edinburgh's cable trams. Car 71 was photographed near the end of the system's life.

For the last two months of operation route 28 was diverted to run by Lauriston, and thus allow reconstruction of the western half of Princes Street. Car 223 turns on to the Mound.

Temporary stop near the top of the Mound – parking created problems for public transport even then!

Completing the climb up the Mound, car 235 crosses the High Street to uplift passengers from the island. Here always pervaded the sweet aroma from Ferguson's Edinburgh Rock works, just off to the left.

Another busy corner for University and Infirmary. The junction of Lauriston Place, Forrest Road and Teviot Place at the top of Middle Meadow Walk during the last year of the trams.

For a short time, while the roadway was being reconstructed, Princes Street had a "reserved track" tramway. Temporary barriers were erected where there was a difference in level. Many well-remembered Princes Street shops can be seen, including Marcus' furriers, with its famous bears (above the second bus on the right).

During the last days of operation, the final decorated tram (former 172) toured the remaining lines. It is seen here at Bruntsfield Links passing number 49 heading for Braids terminus. In the distance, the spire of Barclay Church.

Not much photographed on the last day of operation was old grinder car 3. It was festooned with slogans relating to the contemporary events in troubled Hungary.

The scene at the foot of the Mound with the last car and official party. The event was to have been televised but was so delayed that the allotted time had passed before the procession reached this spot where the official speeches were made. The passing of Edinburgh's trams was watched by thousands, few of whom considered that the correct decision had been made, and few of whom have since had reason to change their minds.

ELECTRIC TRAMWAY ROUTES

Service No.	ROUTE	Route Colour	Service No.	ROUTE	Route Colour
1	LIBERTON AND CORSTORPHINE	RED BLUE	14	CHURCHHILL AND GRANTON CIRCLE *via* Bernard Street	YELLOW GREEN
2	GRANTON AND AND STENHOUSE *via* York Place and George Street	BLUE	15	BRAIDS AND KING'S ROAD *via* York Place and London Road	GREEN WHITE
3	NEWINGTON STN. and STENHOUSE *via* Princes Street	BLUE WHITE	16	BRAIDS AND GRANTON SQUARE *via* York Place, Leith Walk and Junction St.	GREEN
4	PIERSHILL AND SLATEFORD *via* London Road and Princes Street	WHITE BLUE	17	NEWINGTON STN. and GRANTON SQUARE *via* Bernard Street	WHITE
5	MORNINGSIDE STN. Abbeyhill and Piershill *via* Grange Road and Bridges	RED GREEN	18	LIBERTON DAMS AND WAVERLEY *via* Melville Drive and West End	YELLOW WHITE
6	MARCHMONT CIRCLE (Either Direction) Post Office, Marchmont, West End	WHITE RED	19	CRAIGENTINNY AVE. NO. AND TOLLCROSS *via* Bridges & Melville Dr.	GREEN RED
7	LIBERTON AND STANLEY ROAD *via* Junction Street	RED	20	EDINBURGH G.P.O., PORTOBELLO AND JOPPA	RED
8	GRANTON SQUARE and NEWINGTON STN. *via* Broughton Street	RED YELLOW	21	EDINBURGH G.P.O., PORTOBELLO, MUSSELBURGH AND LEVENHALL	GREEN
9	GRANTON SQUARE AND COLINTON *via* Broughton Street	YELLOW	23	GRANTON ROAD STN., TOLLCROSS, BRUNTS-FIELD & MORNINGSIDE *via* Mound	GREEN YELLOW
10	BERNARD STREET AND COLINTON	WHITE YELLOW	24	WAVERLEY STOCKBRIDGE AND COMELY BANK *via* Frederick Street	RED
11	FAIRMILEHEAD AND STANLEY ROAD *via* Pilrig Street	RED WHITE	25	CORSTORPHINE AND CRAIGENTINNY AVENUE NORTH *via* York Place and Leith Walk	BLUE YELLOW
12	CORSTORPHINE KING'S ROAD AND JOPPA *via* Leith and Seafield	YELLOW BLUE	27	GRANTON ROAD STN. AND FIRRHILL *via* Mound and Lauriston	YELLOW RED
13	CHURCHHILL AND GRANTON CIRCLE *via* Pilrig Street	WHITE GREEN		PRIVATE CARS may be engaged for Private Parties—Terms Moderate.	

MOTOR BUS ROUTES

Service No.	ROUTE	Service No.	ROUTE
1	EASTER ROAD (Leith Links), AND CORSTORPHINE *via* STENHOUSE	14	EASTER ROAD (Leith Links), SLATEFORD, KINGSKNOWE AND JUNIPER GREEN
2	CRAIGMILLAR (Hay Drive) AND STENHOUSE *via* Prestonfield Avenue and Gorgie Road	15	EASTFIELD, MILTON ROAD, WILLOWBRAE, TRON CHURCH, CRAIGLOCKHART, COLINTON AND JUNIPER GREEN
3	WAVERLEY (St Andrew Square), CRAIGENTINNY AND PORTOBELLO TOWN HALL	16	PORTOBELLO TOWN HALL, WILLOWBRAE, ARDMILLAN TERRACE AND SIGHTHILL AVENUE
4	EASTER ROAD (Leith Links), SLATEFORD, LONGSTONE AND SIGHTHILL AVENUE	19	WEST END (Randolph Place) AND PILTON (Boswall Loan)
5	WAVERLEY, LOCHEND, BERNARD STREET, STOCKBRIDGE, WEST END, ARDMILLAN TERRACE AND STENHOUSE	21	FAIRMILEHEAD TERMINUS AND HILLEND PARK During Summer Months only Wednesdays Saturdays Sundays } Weather Permitting
6	CRAIGMILLAR (Hay Drive) AND STENHOUSE *via* Cameron Toll and Roseburn	22	COMISTON ROAD (Lodge Gate) AND CITY HOSPITAL Sundays Wednesdays Tuesdays Saturdays
7	WAVERLEY BRIDGE, CRAIGMILLAR, NIDDRIE AND NEWCRAIGHALL	23	WAVERLEY BRIDGE AND EDINBURGH CASTLE (1st April to 30th September only)
8	WAVERLEY BRIDGE, SLATEFORD, KINGSKNOWE AND JUNIPER GREEN	24	POST OFFICE AND MELVILLE STREET (Portobello) Sunday Mornings only (June to September)
9	BLACKHALL, MOUND, BLACKFORD HILL, MORNINGSIDE AND GREENBANK ROAD	25	FOOT OF LEITH WALK AND MORNINGSIDE STATION All Night Service, Monday Nights to Friday Nights inclusive (October to March)
10	PORTOBELLO TOWN HALL, NIDDRIE AND NEWCRAIGHALL	26	ROBERTSON AVENUE AND SALISBURY PLACE All Night Service, Monday Nights to Friday Nights inclusive (October to March)
11	WAVERLEY BRIDGE, BLACK-HALL, DAVIDSON'S MAINS, CRAMOND AND BARNTON		
12	SURGEONS' HALL, CRAIGMILLAR, DUDDINGSTON AND PORTOBELLO TOWN HALL		TRAVEL BY CITY TRANSPORT
13	RAVELSTON DYKES, WEST END, FREDERICK STREET, GREAT KING STREET, LOCHEND AND BERNARD STREET		

For particulars of Motor Coach Tourist Routes, see Apartments Booklet.

TRAVEL BY CITY TRANSPORT

Above: **Tram and bus routes as listed on the 1939 issue of the Transport Department map. Although there were subsequent detail alterations to the tram routes, services added to the list were 22 (route colour blue over blue), a short working from North Junction Street to Stenhouse of route 2; 26 (blue over red), Piershill to Drum Brae, and, in June 1946, 28 (blue over green), a short working from Stanley Road to Braids of route 11.**

ACKNOWLEDGEMENTS

As always, many people have assisted this production, and thanks are due to all of them. In particular I would wish to refer to the late Wm. Allan; and to Messrs I. Cormack, D. Fisher, A. G. Gunn, J. J. Herd, D. Hunt, D. L. G. Hunter; Mrs W. A. Brotchie again transformed manuscript to typescript. Permission to use photographs is recorded with thanks: Collection late Wm. Allan, p.13 top; I. Blair, p.24, p.28, p.36 mid; G. Fairley, p.3, p.19 foot, p.25 top, p.26 top, p.32 top; W. B. Grubb, p.11 mid; D. L. G. Hunter, p.14, p.17 top, p.18 top; R. W. Jones, p.29 foot; Lothian Transport, p.15 foot, p.20, p.21, p.23 mid, p.25 mid, p.26 foot, p.27 mid, p.27 foot, p.30, p.32 foot, p.35 foot, p.37 foot, p.39 foot; R. F. Mack, p.31 top, p.31 mid, p.33, p.34 top, p.36 top, p.36 foot, p. 37 top, p.38 foot; G. Murray, p.13 foot, Old Motor, Cover; late R. B. Parr, p.25 foot, p.27 top, p.29 top; D. C. Thomson Ltd, p.38 top; R. J. S. Wiseman, p.19 mid, p.23 foot, p.34 mid, p.34 foot, p.35 top. All others from N.B. Traction Group Collection.

Printed by Crown Press (Keighley) Limited, Chapel Lane, Keighley, West Yorkshire.